NATIONAL PARKS

A TRUE BOOK

by
David Petersen

Children's Press®
A Division of Scholastic Inc.

New York Toronto London Auckland Sydney
Mexico City New Delhi Hong Kong
Danbury, Connecticut

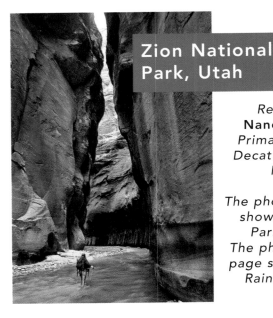

Zion National Park, Utah

Reading Consultant
Nanci R. Vargus, Ed.D.
Primary Multiage Teacher
Decatur Township Schools,
Indianapolis, IN

The photograph on the cover
shows Badlands National
Park in South Dakota.
The photograph on the title
page shows hikers at Mount
Rainier National Park in
Washington.

Visit Children's Press® on the
Internet at:
http://publishing.grolier.com

Library of Congress Cataloging-in-Publication Data

Petersen, David, 1946–
    National parks / by David Petersen.
        p. cm. — (True book)
    Includes bibliographical references and index.
    ISBN 0-516-21667-8   0-516-27321-3 (pbk)
    1. National parks and reserves—United States—Juvenile literature.
2. National parks and reserves—Juvenile literature. [1. National parks and
reserves.] I. Title. II. Series.

SB482.A4P48 2001
333.78'3'0973—dc21   00-030663

©2001 Children's Press®
A Division of Scholastic Inc.
GROLIER
PUBLISHING   1 2 3 4 5 6 7 8 9 10 R 10 09 08 07 06 05 04 03 02 01

Contents

Grand Teton National Park, Wyoming

What Is a Park?

People have created many kinds of parks—amusement parks, ballparks, even car, business, and industrial parks. But for most people, the word "park" means grass, trees, and wild animals— a place to learn and have fun.

In Europe, the first "nature parks" were created centuries

National parks are meant to be enjoyed by everyone.

ago. They were carefully protected, with trees, lakes, grassy meadows, and lots of wildlife. But these parks were privately owned by kings and other royalty, and the public was not allowed in.

In North America today, most nature parks are open to the public. They are owned by all the people of a city, state,

National parks protect natural wonders ranging from glaciers (left) to sand dunes (above).

or nation. They are places where animals are protected and where visitors can walk, run, picnic, camp, swim, and play.

Bryce Canyon National Park in Utah (left) and Crater Lake National Park in Oregon (right)

Olympic National Park, in Washington, is big enough to include mountains, forests (left), and Pacific coastline (right).

Some of the biggest and best parks are called national parks. Around the world today, there are about 1,200 national parks in more than 100 countries. But until 1872, there were none.

"The Best Idea in History"

National parks have been called "the best idea in history." And that idea was born in the United States.

Before 1800, almost no one except American Indians had been west of the Mississippi River. But during the 1800s, the huge, mysterious, western

wilderness was actively explored. One of the earliest explorers was an artist named George Catlin.

In 1832, while sitting on the banks of the Missouri River in what is now South Dakota, George Catlin had "the best idea

George Catlin (left) loved to paint scenes of the Western wilderness.

in history." All around him spread rolling grasslands. Grazing on that sea of grass were great herds of bison, pronghorn, deer, and other wild animals.

Catlin noticed that local Indians were able to live well by hunting these animals and gathering wild plants. Inspired by all of this, Catlin scribbled a daydream in his diary: "What a beautiful and thrilling specimen for America to preserve and hold up to the view of her refined citizens and the world in future ages! A nation's Park, containing man and beast, in all the wild and freshness of their nature's beauty!"

George Catlin's dream did
eventually come true. Almost 150
years later, in 1978, the "wild and
fresh" scene Catlin described
became Badlands National Park.

The First National Park

But George Catlin's Badlands was far from being the country's first national park. That honor went to Yellowstone, in Wyoming.

The Yellowstone story also begins with explorers. For years, fur trappers such as John Colter and Osborne Russell had brought back exciting stories of the strange and lovely country surrounding the Yellowstone River, high in the Rocky Mountains.

Minerva Terrace is one of the unusual natural formations at Yellowstone.

Old Faithful is Yellowstone's most famous geyser.

They told of steaming natural fountains, or geysers, that squirted huge columns of water high in the air. They told of bottomless pools colored

Bacteria and algae color the hot springs at Yellowstone.

like rainbows, and of "mud pots" that bubbled, burped, and smelled like rotten eggs. They spoke of bison, elk, and

Yellowstone's wildlife includes bison (above) and elk (right).

pronghorn by the thousands; of "white" bears (grizzlies) and gigantic moose; of snowcapped mountains and dense green forests; of crystal-clear lakes and streams full of fish. Most of the people who heard these stories called them "tall tales." But the stories kept coming.

In 1870, the Northern Pacific Railroad Company sent a party to explore the Yellowstone region. Six weeks later, the party's leader, Henry Washburn, returned to announce that the "tall tales" all were true!

In 1871, a second team of explorers visited Yellowstone. Its leader was a scientist named Ferdinand V. Hayden. Traveling with Hayden were a photographer named William Henry Jackson and an artist named Thomas Moran.

Months later, in Washington, D.C., members of the U.S. Congress read Hayden's descriptions of the wonders of Yellowstone country, and his pleas that it be protected as a national park. But what impressed those lawmakers most were Jackson's photographs and Moran's paintings of the area.

In 1872, Congress passed the Yellowstone Park Act. It stated

Members of Congress decided that Yellowstone should be made into a national park after seeing Moran's paintings and Jackson's photographs of the region.

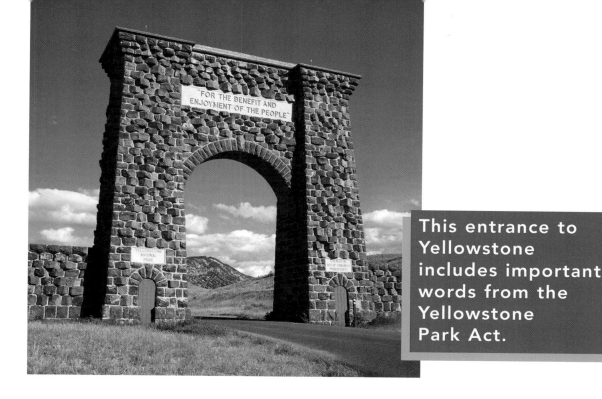

This entrance to Yellowstone includes important words from the Yellowstone Park Act.

that Yellowstone was "reserved and withdrawn from settlement, and dedicated and set apart as a public park or pleasuring-ground for the benefit and enjoyment of the people." The world's first national park was born.

The Father of the National Park System

Just a few years before reports of Yellowstone's natural beauty reached Washington, D.C., another explorer was hiking even farther west. His name was John Muir.

Today, John Muir is remembered as one of America's most

famous nature writers and "the Father of the National Park System." It all started in 1869, when young Muir hiked alone into the Sierra Nevada, a high mountain range in central California.

In the heart of the Sierras, Muir fell in love with the gorgeous valley of the Yosemite River. Everywhere the writer looked, he saw wild nature,

John Muir fell in love with the spectacular Yosemite Valley.

Vernal Falls at Yosemite National Park

freedom, and beauty. Bare rock cliffs soared higher than the tallest city buildings. Thundering waterfalls shook the ground.

Fish swam lazily in sparkling streams. Giant trees bent and danced in the wind. Bears, deer, and other wild animals were Muir's constant companions.

Writing that Yosemite Valley was a place where "nature had gathered her choicest treasures," Muir vowed that someday it would be protected as a national park.

And there was no time to waste. Already, ranching and logging and mining were

Tuolomne Meadows at Yosemite National Park (above), and winter light at Yosemite (right)

gnawing away at the Sierras, threatening to spoil their delicate beauty. Fighting back,

Muir wrote books and magazine stories about the wonders of Yosemite. He also tried to interest important friends in creating a national park.

Twenty-one years later, in 1890, Muir's dream finally came true. Yosemite National Park was created.

Over the years that followed, John Muir worked with his friend, President Theodore Roosevelt, to help create other national parks.

The National Park System Today

By 2000, the American National Park System had grown to include 378 parks, monuments, and other special places. There are National Park sites in 49 of the 50 United States, the District of Columbia, American Samoa, Guam, Puerto Rico, Saipan, and the Virgin Islands.

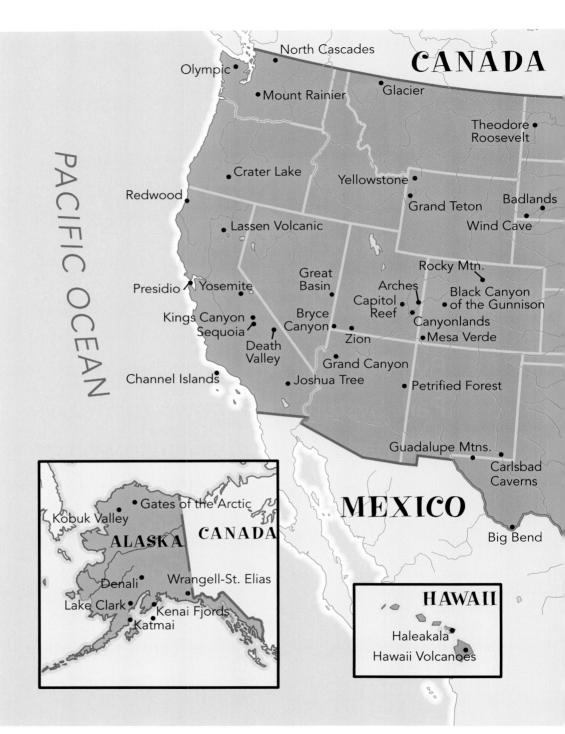

PACIFIC OCEAN

CANADA

North Cascades

Olympic

Mount Rainier

Glacier

Theodore
Roosevelt

Crater Lake

Yellowstone

Badlands

Redwood

Grand Teton

Wind Cave

Lassen Volcanic

Rocky Mtn.

Great
Basin

Arches

Black Canyon
of the Gunnison

Presidio

Yosemite

Capitol
Reef

Kings Canyon
Sequoia

Bryce
Canyon

Canyonlands

Mesa Verde

Death
Valley

Zion

Channel Islands

Grand Canyon

Joshua Tree

Petrified Forest

Guadalupe Mtns.

Carlsbad
Caverns

MEXICO

Big Bend

Gates of the Arctic

Kobuk Valley

ALASKA

CANADA

Denali

Wrangell-St. Elias

Lake Clark

Kenai Fjords

Katmai

HAWAII

Haleakala

Hawaii Volcanoes

NATIONAL PARKS
OF THE
UNITED STATES

Voyageurs
Isle Royale

Acadia

UNITED STATES

Shenandoah•

•Mammoth Cave

•Great Smoky Mtns.

Hot Springs•

ATLANTIC OCEAN

N
W • E
S

Alaska

Hawaii

Virgin Islands

American Samoa

Biscayne
Dry Tortugas• Everglades

Grand Canyon National Park, Arizona (left), and Virgin Islands National Park (above)

Together, they preserve 80.7 million acres (32.7 million hectares) of land.

America's biggest national park is in America's biggest state. Wrangell-St. Elias National Park in Alaska preserves 13.2 million acres

Wrangell-St. Elias National Park, Alaska

(5.3 million hectares) of wilderness, along with many species of wildlife.

The smallest unit in the National Park System is Thaddeus Kosciuszko National Memorial, in Pennsylvania. It's no larger than a school playground!

Park or Monument— What's the Difference?

National parks preserve a combination of features, including scenery, wildlife, and historical sites. They are created by the U.S. Congress. The U.S. now has 54 national parks.

National monuments protect one main feature. Monuments are created by the president of the United States. There are 73 national monuments.

▲ Great Smoky Mountains National Park, Tennessee and North Carolina

▲ Haleakala National Park, Hawaii

▼ Everglades National Park, Florida

▲ Statue of Liberty
National Monument, New
Jersey and New York

▲ Martin Luther King, Jr.,
National Memorial, Georgia

**Other National
Park System classifica-
tions include memori-
als, battlefields, historic
sites, seashores, rivers,
preserves, scenic trails,
and more.**

▲ Gettysburg National
Military Park, Pennsylvania

Cape Hatteras National
Seashore, North Carolina ▼

Rio Grande Wild and
Scenic River, Texas ▼

Parks, People— and Problems

America's national parks now host an average of 270 million visits per year. That's more people than attend all professional U.S. sporting events—football, baseball, basketball, and the rest—combined.

But people aren't the biggest problem—cars are. Cars cause

Hikers at Glacier National Park, Montana (above) and summer traffic at Zion National Park, Utah (left)

traffic jams, make noise, and foul the air with fumes. Cars frighten and kill wildlife and frustrate visitors.

The car problem is so serious in some popular parks—including Yosemite in California and Denali in Alaska—that visitors must now park their cars at the entrance and tour the parks on foot, bicycle, or public transportation.

And this is good. One of the best ways to enjoy nature is on foot—just like the early explorers!

Denali National Park, Alaska

No matter who you are or where you live, America's national parks are yours. Enjoy them often, and do your part

Canyonlands National Park, Utah

to preserve them for the future. Someday you'll want your children to be able to say that national parks are still "the best idea in history."

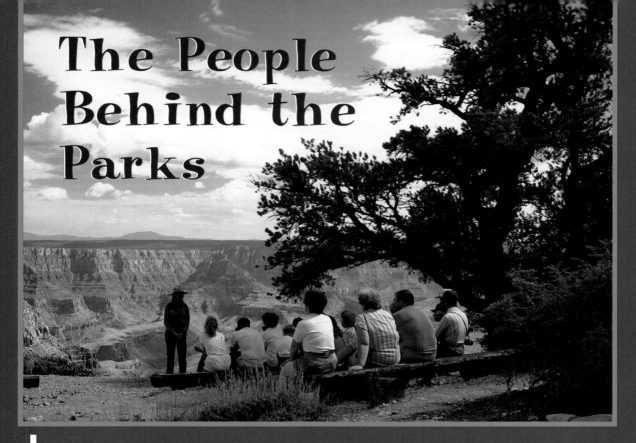

The People Behind the Parks

It takes lots of people to make our National Park System work. Business managers, biologists, maintenance people, and shopkeepers all work for the national parks.

The best-known park employees are the rangers. Park rangers are also called "interpreters." They lead nature hikes, give campfire talks, enforce park rules, and otherwise help visitors have a safe, fun time.

To Find Out More

Here are some additional resources to help you learn more about national parks:

Books

Halverson, Lisa. **Letters Home from Yosemite.** Blackbirch Marketing, 2000.

Petersen, David. **Yellowstone National Park.** Children's Press, 2001.

Tesar, Jenny E. **America's Top 10 National Parks.** Blackbirch Marketing, 1998.

Weber, Michael. **Our National Parks.** Millbrook Press, 1995.

Organizations and Online Sites

Greater Yellowstone Coalition

http://www.greater yellowstone.org/

Find out how you can help protect America's first national park.

National Parks Conservation Association

1300 Nineteenth St. NW Washington, D. C. 20036

An organization founded to help protect the nation's parks for future generations.

National Park Service: ParkNet

http://www.nps.gov/

For official information on the National Park Service, with links to all national park websites.

Yosemite Online

http://yosemite.org/

Includes visitor information, a history of the park, a virtual tour, and a live webcam photograph of Yosemite Valley that is refreshed every 3 minutes.

Important Words

bison also called buffalo; large, shaggy, wild member of the cattle family

classification division into types or categories

companions friends

foul make dirty

gorgeous extremely beautiful

massive huge

plains flat grasslands

preserve to save and keep unchanged

pronghorn wild, goatlike animal of the western prairies

species a specific kind of plant or animal

specimen sample

wilderness area of undeveloped land where nature is left unchanged

Index

Meet the Author

David Petersen has been writing True Books for more than a third of his life, including many titles in the National Parks and Monuments series. David, who lives in Colorado, says he feels that it's his "duty and privilege as an American" to visit national parks, monuments, and other public lands of the United States as often as possible.